# Frugal Living

# When Less Means More

Fhilcar Faunillan

Mendon Cottage Books

*JD-Biz Publishing*

**Disclaimer**

The information is this book is provided for informational purposes only. It is not intended to be used and medical advice or a substitute for proper medical treatment by a qualified health care provider. The information is believed to be accurate as presented based on research by the author.

The contents have not been evaluated by the U.S. Food and Drug Administration or any other Government or Health Organization and the contents in this book are not to be used to treat cure or prevent disease.

The author or publisher is not responsible for the use or safety of any diet, procedure or treatment mentioned in this book. The author or publisher is not responsible for errors or omissions that may exist.

**Warning**

The Book is for informational purposes only and before taking on any diet, treatment or medical procedure, it is recommended to consult with your primary health care provider.

Our books are available at

1. Amazon.com
2. Barnes and Noble
3. Itunes
4. Kobo
5. Smashwords
6. Google Play Books

# Table of Contents

# Chapter 1: Introduction to Frugal Living

What comes into your mind when you first hear about frugal living? You may be one of the many people who are likely to utter the words such as cheap lifestyle, miserable life, boring, or unhappy life. However, frugal living does not mean any of those words. It is not a miserable way of life because it is a choice in the first place because no one ever chooses to live a miserable life. More so, it is not boring considering the number of meaningful activities one could engage in when living in frugality. And more than that, frugal living does not mean having an unhappy life because it only means finding happiness beyond what money could offer.

Surely, money allows you to buy the things you need, or maybe gain significant experiences. However, with the consumerist lifestyle that most people have, there is a greater tendency to consume more, and spend for what is useless in life. Most people do not even realize that there is an abundance of ways to get to experience what they want in life. Instead, they go for expensive materials and buy those with big brand names, or get a luxury vacation package, and then show it off for others to see because it is what has been taught to them.

When we talk about frugal living, we are dealing with a free lifestyle. It also means untying from a societally controlled lifestyle, which is the root of many of the pressing issues today. With the overly mindless consumption and consumerist lifestyle that most people have, we could say that the world desperately needs to learn the principles of frugal living. The proof of this frantic need for change is seen every day, when you see people drive to work in their single-occupied SUVs, whizz at the sight of beers and pack of cigarettes that minimum wage workers feast on during the day, or the group of youth holding their smartphones barely talking to each other. Regardless of your family's income levels, no one is immune to mindless consumption and no one is exempted from rejecting frugality.

Most people fail to pursue frugal living, even at the micro and macro levels. The United States economy is falling at the pit of debt, which is thrice the GNP of Japan, yet the country continues to spend more. And for the information of everybody, Japan has the world's third largest economy. That makes it so unbelievable how we confidently spend money, while also watching a handful of European countries worry about debt and everything combined. And it is not so surprising that this consumerist behavior reflects the spending behavior of most of its people.

Fortunately, at present, there is a growing return to frugal living, given the condition and the aftermath of the Great Recession. The unemployment rates serve as a wake-up call for proper execution of our financial responsibilities.

# Frugal Living as a Choice

Frugality often falls in two categories. There are people who live frugally because their financial situation dictates so, whereas others live frugally because it is their choice. The latter is a thoughtful decision to live simply and become conscious of their spending. This would mean lesser wasted resources, enjoying more time for themselves and others, and become more satisfied in life.

America has its history of the Great Depression, where embracing a frugal living was a necessity. The people had no other choice but to make the most out of what they have. There was basically almost nothing. The people could not choose how to live their lives because they only thought about having to survive. But today, people can choose what to do and what not. For most people, frugal living becomes a choice, and a decisive commitment to a simple way of life. These people have chosen to fix rather than buy a new one, living below the means, and having more time for social relationships. It would also mean untangling from technology, getting back to ordinary living, gardening, having a small home, and enjoy more with people.

Choosing to have a frugal life is not easy. It takes enough self-control, given that we know it is always less of a hassle to buy new things when something gets broken, get instant gratification, and then worry about the payment later. It also takes enough self-discipline to remain patient, to fix broken things, to think about the things you need, and to save more money for something greater. These are just some of the many challenges when committing to live in frugality.

# Frugality as a State of Mind

Being successful in your choice to live frugally does not directly attack your spending behavior. First, you have to condition your mind and set it according to the principles of frugal living, and the rest will follow.

Living frugally is more than just making the necessary efforts to save more money. It is also more than just a way of living. In other words, frugal living is a state of mind. It entails bargaining to get what you want while also saving money. It is also being able to realize that there are bigger and more important things in life than material possessions. When you have been accustomed to this way of life, you will realize that these materials are adversative to a simple and happy living.

Frugal living also necessitates weighing of opportunity costs. You simply can't have everything all at once. But that is not something to feel bad about, because later on, you will realize that life is much more enjoyable when you live it at a slower pace. You will feel that there is peace by simply relaxing at the front porch and listening to the silence, or enjoying the old board games with family more than being caught in different directions with mobile phones, fancy expensive bags, and other vices.

Frugal living also encourages people to be knowledgeable with do-it-yourself projects. Ignorance may be bliss, but it could also be very expensive. When we talk about frugal living, there is no room for huge ignorance. For example, if you do not know how to design a home that would cut electricity costs, then that would mean higher monthly bills. It is important to learn different DIY projects and other ways to get things without having to shell out big amounts of money. Another example would be realizing that a packed lunch from home would mean lower cost than eating at a fast food chain or any other restaurants; or when you realize that SUVs are not necessary to get somewhere and that a Toyota Corolla will do.

As you go through life having a frugal mindset, you will learn that those who drive luxury cars or collect designer bags for reasons of showing off are just shallow drips you do not have to be impressed with, in the same way that living in a simple home is a wiser decision than moving to have a bigger house at a high-end neighborhood or simply outgrowing a house is pure nonsense. Living frugally is removing all pretentions and moving up from being fixated on designer bags, expensive cars, or big houses. Putting all things together, you will get to see that frugal living a solution to most of our problems.

# Living Frugally Doesn't Mean Leaving the Fun

Frugal living does not necessarily mean you have to leave the fun behind. Whereas some people think you have to wear simple clothes, own simple stuff, or live in an exaggeratedly small home to be frugal, that is still not the main point. Living frugally only entails being good at finding ways to save money and avoid large debts, prepare retirement funds earlier, and invest on something to have it work for you. Some may live frugally to get a short vacation to Europe, add a sunroom to their home, or buy a new pair of shoes. But whatever the reason may be, the point is that you have to understand that living frugally does not equate to having a boring life. It is just about saving money while still having fun.

Instead of focusing on what you should do without, shift your emphasis from material possessions and save your money or spend more time with the people around you. When you do this, you will see that living a frugal life is fun and profitable. Here are some of the frugal principles you can adapt in your daily life:

- Find ways to save money daily
- Start a savings plan
- Set your goals and purpose so you know exactly what you are working for
- Increase your income doing the things you like
- Don't be a wage slave
- Improve bargaining and haggling skills

When you have committed to having a frugal lifestyle, you will see it could be fun trying to find ways to get to your long-term and short-term goals. There are actually many fun things to do without having to break the banks.

You can engage in a local community center to learn something new, join free classes, or get involved in recreational activities in the community. You could also take some volunteering opportunities to help those in need while also having a rewarding feeling from being able to help. You can take part in community gardening or other activities for providing for animal shelter. Public parks are also great places to relax with family. You can also go to museums where there are free admissions and enjoy the exhibits. Experiment on new meals at home, read more books from book sales, or grow your own food by starting your own garden. This will save you money for food and you will be proud you served your dinner with ingredients coming from your own garden. You can even build a small home where you could live more closely with family.

Again, being frugal does not equate misery. It is enjoying the simplest things in life and freeing oneself from material slavery. It is doing things that involve lesser amount of money, while still being able to enjoy in life.

# Chapter 2: What the Great Depression Has Taught Us

Those who have survived from the Great Depression certainly have lessons to impart and hold for the rest of their lives. At one point, they were able to live frugally because it was the only choice. During this period in the 1930s, people had farms and were greatly diverse. Various crops were grown organically, as well as vegetables and fruits. Home-gardening was very common. The raising of chickens, hogs, cattle, horses, and sheep enabled individuals to survive. Also, farmers kept bees so they could harvest honey later on. Women, on the other hand, baked bread for meals.

It was during the Great Depression when self-sufficiency practices were carried over and adopted by individuals into their own social lives. Suppers were usually one-dish and potlucks were maintained so people could still have fun while sharing their foods. Radio and magazines talked about how people should stretch their budget by suggesting meals that would save them more money, such as toasts, waffles, soups, biscuits, and chipped beef.

However, in the years that followed the Great Depression, so much has changed in the country. People started to upgrade their way of living and passed this lifestyle to the next generation, which is why it is not so surprising why so many people live so extravagantly. The people have been accustomed to living more comfortably, and in the easiest way they could think of, not knowing that frugal living is the best way to do so.

# Chapter 3: Today's Lifestyle: Mindless and Consumerist

Individuals are in a cycle of impulsive spending behavior, splurging so much when there is little money, for things that they don't really need, and to impress people who do not even care. The messages that the society tells us, from the government, to the media, economists, and a lot of sources had the people believe that being good consumers means buying more stuff. These sources encourage people to buy more because it would mean supporting people in their jobs. It is just a bunch of nonsense.

The current lifestyle involves greater spending because it is what has been taught to people. The society has set a standard lifestyle of which to follow. It has set a 40-hour work week lifestyle where people become a bunch of slaves working for the people up there and help them get richer. This is not to say that working for bosses is entirely wrong. It becomes wrong when we work just to satisfy our material thirst. Working for 40 hours a week apparently lessens the time spent with family, and so people kill their pockets on the weekends by spending so much for a night out or buy things to make them happy. When they get a raise in pay, they also tend to spend more and upgrade their lifestyle. There is an undying cycle of spending together with the increase in pay.

It is about time that we stop giving in to these messages the government, the media, economists, and many other sources have been constantly feeding us. Even before indulging in another spending activity, always think about how its consumption will affect you and whether you have exercised mindful consumption when you decided to make a purchase. Throughout the years, individuals have displayed mindless and consumerist behavior and it is high time to change this. This kind of behavior affects us and others negatively and in so many ways possible. If this behavioral problem is not remedied today, this extravagant lifestyle may prosper in the generations that will follow.

# Chapter 4: How Society Has Conditioned Our Current Lifestyles

There is a long history of the country's economic meltdown, along with an overt focus of individuals' spending behavior. Savings have turned down from 11% to below zero, while filing of bankruptcies has skyrocketed since 1982. Debts rose to huge amounts and several reasons have been worded to explain why individuals have this overspending behavior. Research findings suggest that effective advertising, as well as quick cultural shifts encouraging consumerism were strong forces that strengthened this trend of spending. And so every time individuals get the urge to spend, and because they are capable of doing so, they tend to act on these impulsively. This only poses greater challenge for the people.

Society has conditioned the people to act in a specific way. And because individuals are highly flexibly animals who are naturally inclined to conform to the society, they tend to give in to society's demands and crash out the self-control. There are numerous factors that play within and around us that influence the way we spend. Just like the muscle that gets tired after too much physical activity, it tends to deplete its resources and therefore fail in completing its tasks. In the case of human beings, when a depletion of resources happens, there is no more energy to think and exert self-control. In real situations, people in the work force are bombarded with demands and are often caught under stress, deadlines, bad relationships, which only increase the tendency to display excessive spending behavior.

In another instance, credit cards encourage and condition people to build up debt. In the past, there was a deregulation of the interest rates in credit card and only the affluent people qualified to get one. The industry rises again by soliciting more consumers and offering credit with high interest rates without setting financial qualifications or even a guide on how to use these properly. A research from the Journal of Consumer Research suggest that these credit cards only increase the probability of people giving in to their impulses and worry about getting the purchases paid later on.

Our society tells us to spend! Millions were funded for strategic advertising and marketing especially in big businesses. They also do research on how they could induce people to make more purchases. Before, people were not commercial animals in their own homes. But now, with the advent of technology, catalogs, toll-free phones, as well as the internet, it has been easier for advertisers to reach out to their target market, and it has become easier for people to easily spend their paychecks. People can shop online, call to place an order, and be exposed to TV commercials and other shopping outlets. Whereas advertisements used to be in magazines and newspapers, now they are found everywhere you look. Stickers, billboards, wall ads, flyers, and other forms of media are all around to tell you to buy their product.

The most troublesome about these forms of media is that they are effective in persuading people to consume more. These are mostly the reasons that drive people into debt, and worse, unhappiness. Financial difficulties have been a common problem to many American families. It has also been the root of stresses and depressions. Several researches have linked these financial difficulties to absenteeism, lower productivity and other illnesses among people.

It is high time to bring back the principles of frugal living and restore the old simple lifestyle. Compared to people from the past, the people today have more material possessions and they tend to feast in its abundance. But no matter how much possessions they have, many of them are deeply miserable. It is definitely a time to call for the old way of life.

# Chapter 5: Small House Living

When you think about the trend of the world's economy and how it has moved in instability for the past decade, you may think about a reassessment of your own life situation. How does this trend affect you in the near future? Will you possibly lose your job when you don't expect it? Will you be able to pay the mortgage to keep a home for your family? It would be great to ask these kinds of questions and take careful planning on what you could do to prepare for the huge unknowns of our future economy. There is no magic when it comes to the inevitable course of our future. It is all up to us. What could happen to the world a few years from now?

With much of the world's resources being exploited and squandered at a fast rate, these are important thoughts to ponder upon. Before engaging in big financial decisions in life such as the mortgage of your house, the area where you will live, the type of energy resource you will use, always study the question 'Am I possibly going to go through a financial storm like what the world is going through right now?' Always take your time to decide on these choices, view the endless possibilities in different lenses, and cope up with the rapidly changing world to avoid getting crippled to financial strain in the future.

There are many ways to exercise frugal living. Some are big ways and some are small. Let's dig deeper on to one of the bigger ways to display frugality. One of the very big investments most individuals plan on making in their lives is investing on a house. Not most people have awoken to the great alternative of having a small house. It is certainly an excellent housing option for people who want to keep up with the changing economy. It is beneficial in so many ways:

- By replacing your expensive mortgage with smaller ones, you can save greater amount of money. For one, it will save you from high interest rates. In another way, it will save you from greater debts because building or buying a smaller house only utilizes few materials.

- Having a small house will open windows for more alternative resources in energy, utility bills, and the like.

- When you have a small house, you also start to think about the small things, and practice small ways of frugal living. Having a small house does not entitle you to fill blank spaces with so many items you do not need. In effect, this will help you save money for more experiences, instead of buying more and more things which you only thought you needed.

# Saying NO To Expensive Home Loans

It is not impossible to live large even when in small places. In a small house living, houses are built to emphasize space by using innovative and cheaper methods to turn down a huge mortgage. In fact, one can build a house even without having mortgage at all.

Maintaining a DIY in change of housing for a simpler living is a good option when you want a frugal living. You can plan on making smaller homes at many accessible places. There are also micro homes which could help you minimize your mortgage expenses or simply build your house with no mortgage and invest the excess fund for better use. By simply cutting back whatever is in excess and becoming better in finding ways to utilize resources is the start of smart living.

Is your mortgage taking so much portion of your monthly income? Are you left with a very small amount of money after paying your bills? Have you thought about how financially stable you would be if you didn't have such huge mortgage to maintain? By living large in your small house, you could start living your dream of becoming financially free from loans and other forms of debts, which means less stress and more free time for yourself and significant others.

Apart from the abovementioned benefits, there are more reasons why you should forget about the expensive home loan. First of all, the income you get from your job is not always a guarantee. Many workers have experienced lay-offs when they least expect it and as the trend shows, there is continuous economic depression. More so, home loans involve interest rates which are not fixed throughout the repayment process. The amount you pay by the time you bought your house may multiply to shocking numbers if the bank wants to increase the interest rates. Some people are forced to work multiple jobs just to keep up with the home loan. These financial stresses also keep you from enjoying your life debt free. It could lessen the time you spend with loved ones, and if you have a hobby, you may not have the time to do so because you needed to work. If the bank says they need their money, despite being in financial crisis, the bank will take in any means anything from you. Whereas the banks may seem helpful especially for people who have bad credit line, they are not really giving you a favor. Those with bad credit histories are given higher interest rates compared to standard ones because these people are posing a risk to the bank.

The idea of huge mortgages help you realize and reassess your financial situation to determine whether you are still going to go for a home mortgage. When you properly plan and build your house, and take less space, you are more likely to cancel out expensive electricity and gas costs. More so, you can cut down your expenses for housework. When taken seriously, shifting from having a big house to a smaller one does not only change space size, but also your lifestyle and mindset. This time, your living habits shift from spending to saving money.

In reality, small houses are more effective ways of reducing mortgages and other repayments. Most big housing plans take great chunks from the annual income. If you want lesser mortgage or no mortgage at all, you can do the following to help you get your small and eco-friendly house:

- Look for house plans that are smaller, but would comfortably fit you and your family.
- You can always build a house and have lesser, or, be free of mortgage. You do not have to build the house on your own. There are many solutions for non-DIYers alike. By having a small house built for yourself, it will already save you thousands of bucks.

- Only look after small spaces enough to house your family and your pets comfortably. There are always spaces for them.

- By living in smaller homes, you become more creative and dynamic, as you start to engage in small DIY activities to make your home conducive place to live in. You are free to furnish your house in small packages.

- You can design your own home to make it cost-efficient. You may design your house to enable the use of natural lighting or utilization of clean energy sources.

- You may also include a small garden to grow your foods and become independent of what is available in the market. This will save you much money on your daily meals.

- Remember that by going small, you are not forgoing the pleasures of luxury. A small house plan could create a storm of mind shifts.

---

# Other Benefits of Small House Living

For some people, living in a small house may sound like a challenge. With the lifestyle that we have been conditioned to for the past decades, this is certainly a sort of test which forces us to think further, and be innovative in the way we deal with this lifestyle. Living in a small space challenges you how to fit your belongings in a manner that does not over-occupy your space, be fantastic in welcoming guests to your home, and decorating it to whichever is fancy for you.

If you are living frugally because it was your choice, or by any other circumstance which forced you to do so, think about the benefits of frugal living and the positive things you could get from it.

First of all, living in small houses allows you to utilize whatever things you have. You only use the things you need and therefore no space is wasted. Tables, chairs, shelves, and closets are all used, and there is no overstoring of unimportant stuff. Moreover, living in a small house leaves you less for cleaning. Cleaning the house would be a little less stressful than running up and down the stairs or moving around big spaces carrying a vacuum. In addition, you could free yourself from the heavy burden of utility bills. Monthly bills take up chunks of one's income. Bills are everywhere, but when you live in a small house, you are taking a step towards minimizing these bills. Power usage could go down and electric bills could be as low as $40 per month, given that there are lesser rooms to heat or light. Also, living in a small house makes you think more creatively and dynamically. You can position the different rooms according to your preference, maximize your assets, and furnish home spaces. Hosting guests also takes your skill to a higher level by brainstorming of ways to welcome and accommodate them into your home. Being so close to each other while staying at home only leaves a blast of the event and certainly lots of fun. Furthermore, living frugally by having a smaller house keeps you balance all your wants and needs. It forces you to think about the price tag attached to a large population and how silly it is to add unused rooms or store other unimportant stuff in your house. It throws you a question of what you want and what you really need. If you don't need a big house, then do not get one. If you are happy and satisfied with having a home that ties you to your family, have plenty of foods on the table and enough spaces where you could exercise your hobbies, then just be it.

# Conclusion

Frugal living is not entirely being a cheapskate or any other negative connotation you may have associated with it. It is simply about being clever and smart in the way you deal with financial matters. It is about being meticulous in the purchases you make, the properties you plan to get, the management of budget, investments, and most importantly, being mindful about the negativity of buying in to different forms of debts.

More specifically, frugal living attacks the way you think and the way you spend. Its principles exist to move the people to revolutionize from consumerism. Because of billions worth of ads, people are brainwashed to think that the product is effective in making us happy and satisfied. However, this is not how reality should be. One can get a good quality product at lower costs, independent of what is available in store. The best quality of materials is not always found in malls or what have you. Ensuring the transparency and credibility of the goods are always a requirement for great investments.

There is an ultimate goal behind the strong force which pushes us to live frugally, and that is to achieve financial stability, independence, as well as security as early as possible, and having ample of time to maintain it. This driving force eventually leads us to living a high quality life. By simply being informed of what the things that you should do, and by having the knowledge regarding financial matters and smart living, you are in control of the game.

As you end reading this book, you will learn that it takes a good mindset to start living fruitfully. Once you experience the benefits of frugal living, you will be inspired to do more and become an inspiration to more people.

# Author Bio

**Fhilcar Faunillan**

Born in the central part of the Philippines, Fhilcar Faunillan developed her interest in a lot of things – pets, gardening, urban and rural living, prepping, culinary and travel. There she finished her business and law degree and spent some years teaching in college while doing some business of sorts.

Her love for writing and sharing her experiences, doing charitable works and exploring new ideas as well as extending help to children whose basic education needs to be assisted never ceased as she is in the process of putting up her own learning center.

Fhilcar's horizon seems limitless as she embraces the changes around her but critically thinks of their practical relevance.

Check out some of the other JD-Biz Publishing books

Gardening Series on Amazon

# Health Learning Series

Amazing Animal Book Series

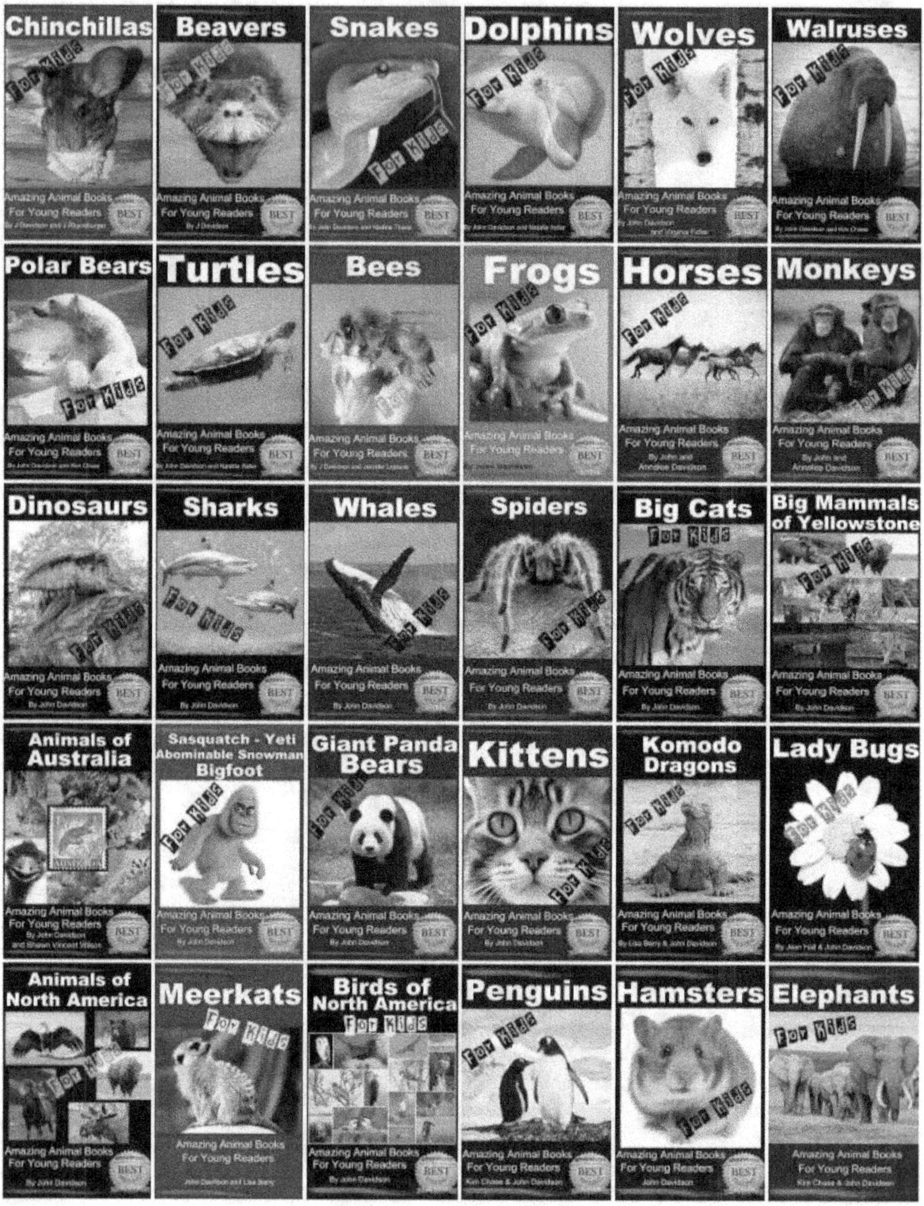

# Learn To Draw Series

# How to Build and Plan Books

# Entrepreneur Book Series

Our books are available at

1. Amazon.com

2. Barnes and Noble

3. Itunes

4. Kobo

5. Smashwords

6. Google Play Books

# Publisher

JD-Biz Corp

P O Box 374

Mendon, Utah 84325

http://www.jd-biz.com/